M

Nelson Mandela

LEADING THE WAY

jB-Mandela /H

rth

Consultants

Timothy Rasinski, Ph.D.
Kent State University

Lori Oczkus
Literacy Consultant

Nelson Mandela Centre of Memory

Based on writing from
TIME For Kids. *TIME For Kids* and the *TIME For Kids* logo are registered trademarks of TIME Inc. Used under license.

Publishing Credits
Dona Herweck Rice, *Editor-in-Chief*
Lee Aucoin, *Creative Director*
Jamey Acosta, *Senior Editor*
Lexa Hoang, *Designer*
Stephanie Reid, *Photo Editor*
Rane Anderson, *Contributing Author*
Rachelle Cracchiolo, *M.S.Ed., Publisher*

Image Credits: cover, pp.1, 23 (top), 35, 43 Newscom; pp.11, 48 Associate Press; pp.22, 30 AFP/Getty Images; pp.5 (both), 6, 10,12–14 (left) Getty Images; p.39 Time & Life Pictures/Getty Images; pp.28–29, 36 (right) iStockphoto; pp.24, 31, 45 AFP/ Getty Images/Newscom; pp.15 (top), 18–19, 23 (bottom), 25 (right), 27 (top), 29 akg-images/Newscom; p.27 (middle) DanitaDelimont.com/Newscom; pp.3, 34, 38 Reuters/Newscom; p.17 Photo Researchers, Inc.; pp.8–9, 20–21, 24–25, 40–41 Timothy J. Bradley & Grace Alba; All other images from Shutterstock.

Teacher Created Materials
5301 Oceanus Drive
Huntington Beach, CA 92649-1030
http://www.tcmpub.com
ISBN 978-1-4333-4864-8
© 2013 Teacher Created Materials, Inc.

Table of Contents

Chapter 1

A Leader Is Born

The world is filled with people of diverse backgrounds. People around the world look different. They have different ideas. They come from different places. But people are alike in many ways, too. And every human being deserves fair and equal treatment. There are many people in this world who stand up for this idea.

Nelson Mandela is one of those people. He fought for **equality**. He believed people can live in peace even if they are different. Mandela worked hard to make South Africa a fair place. He never gave up, even in the worst of times. With the help of others, he built a **democracy**. Today, he is known as the Father of South African Freedom.

THINK LINK

- Who is Nelson Mandela?
- How did he bring freedom to his country?
- Why does he inspire so many people today?

A Young African

Mandela was born on July 18, 1918. He lived in the small village of Qunu. As a young boy, he helped his parents with chores. He was the first in his family to attend school.

The land Mandela's family lived on was owned by the state. White people made laws in South Africa. Africans could not own land. But there were few white people in Qunu. As a child, Mandela knew very little about the relations between white and black people.

Try This

The village name *Qunu* comes from a traditional African language. To say the word, place the tip of your tongue right behind your teeth at the top of your mouth. Keep your mouth round and draw your tongue down quickly to make a *click* sound. The rest of the word is pronounced *oo-hoo*.

South Africa 1970

Legend:
- White
- Mixed Heritage
- African

Mandela's South Africa

South Africa is a country of many different people and cultures. Africans are the biggest group of people. There are also many **minority** groups, including Khoisan, Indians, whites, and people of mixed race.

As a child, Mandela liked building toy animals out of clay. He even used tree branches to make an ox pulling a sleigh.

A Man of Many Names

How many names do you have? Most people have a first name, a middle name, and a last name. Sometimes, we have nicknames, too. Nelson Mandela is a man of many names. Each of his names has a unique meaning and a story to go with it.

Dalibhunga

Madiba

"Aaah! Dalibhunga," people say to Mandela in greeting. He was given this name at the age of 16, when he became a man. The name means "creator or founder of the council."

Mandela is a member of the Madiba clan. In Africa, it is polite to call a person by his or her clan name. Using this name tells others of Mandela's **ancestry**.

Rolihlahla

Mandela's father gave him the name *Rolihlahla* at birth. It means "to pull a branch from a tree." Others translate the name as "troublemaker." Despite his name, Mandela was a kind and obedient child.

Nelson

A teacher gave Nelson this name on the first day of school. It was common for teachers to give the children in their class English names.

Tata

Tata means "father." Many people call him *Tata* because they respect and admire Mandela as much as their own fathers.

Khulu

Mandela is called *Khulu* by his grandchildren. Khulu is the shortened form of *Tat'omkhulu*, which means "grandfather."

9

Tribal Truths

Mandela's father was a chief. He died when Mandela was young. Mandela went to live with a relative. This man was the *regent*, or person acting as king, of the Thembu people. This is where Mandela learned about politics. The regent talked about the affairs of the tribe. He worked hard to meet the needs of his people and tried to be a good leader. Mandela's father and the Thembu regent taught him how to be fair-minded. They showed him how to bring people together. At an early age, Mandela learned how to be a good leader.

a traditional wedding ceremony

Mandela's father was a chief of the Thembu people.

Nelson Mandela with Oliver Tambo

Signs of a Leader

Once in college, Mandela joined the Students' Representative Council. But Mandela and the council soon learned that they had little power to improve student life. The school refused many of their requests. In response, Mandella **boycotted** council elections. The school told Mandela and Oliver Tambo, his friend and fellow activist, to leave.

Arranged Marriages

When Mandela was 22, his family made a plan for him to be married. It was common for **royals** to have arranged marriages. They are not based on two people being in love. They are made to unite communities. In arranged marriages, families often exchange land and money.

Chapter 2

Confronting Apartheid

Mandela wanted to obey his family. But that didn't mean he was ready to get married. So he ran away. He went to the capital city. It was very different from where Mandela had lived. He saw how unfairly Africans were treated. There were rules that kept them out of parks and movie theaters. Whites were allowed inside. But Africans were not. Mandela didn't think this was fair. There were even separate areas where Africans had to live. These areas had no running water. There were no clean streets. There were no beautiful schools.

Mandela knew he wanted to change the laws. He wanted to be a lawyer. His friend Walter Sisulu helped him get a job at a law firm. As his father's son, Mandela had the right to be a chief. But he gave up his position. He went to school instead. After years of study, he became a lawyer.

African National Congress

Sisulu was a member of the African National Congress (ANC). The group was working hard to make South Africa a democracy. They worked to change laws and to educate people. Sisulu invited Mandela to join the group. Later, the ANC helped Mandela become president.

Walter Sisulu

Evelyn Mandela

Marriage

While he was studying to become a lawyer, Mandela married Evelyn Mase. She was Walter Sisulu's cousin. Mase and Mandela had four children together, but Mandela's work made it difficult for them to be a family. They later divorced. He later married Winnie Madikizela (ma-dee-kee-ZAY-lah). They remained together from 1958 to 1992. He has been married to Graça Machel since 1998.

an ANC rally

A Dangerous Position

From 1948 to 1994, the National Party government ruled South Africa. The National Party started the system of **apartheid** (uh-PAHRT-heyt). It made racial **segregation** law. Under apartheid, it was legal for whites to treat Africans unfairly.

Mandela wanted to change the laws. He believed **peaceful protests** could help change these unfair practices. He didn't want to fight or hurt people. He wanted people to talk. He thought they could find a way to agree. Most people in the government didn't believe in doing things that way. They avoided talking. They didn't want to share their power. Instead, they arrested or hurt people who opposed them. This put Mandela in danger. He wanted to help Africans. But if he did, he could be arrested or worse.

Mandela in his office

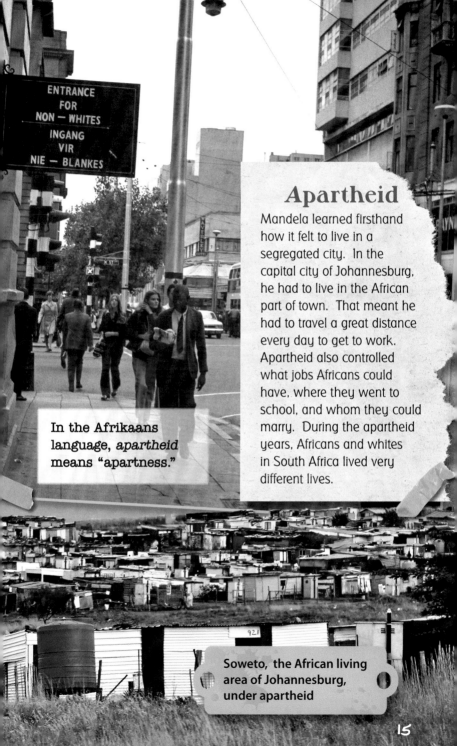

ENTRANCE
FOR
NON – WHITES
INGANG
VIR
NIE – BLANKES

Apartheid

Mandela learned firsthand how it felt to live in a segregated city. In the capital city of Johannesburg, he had to live in the African part of town. That meant he had to travel a great distance every day to get to work. Apartheid also controlled what jobs Africans could have, where they went to school, and whom they could marry. During the apartheid years, Africans and whites in South Africa lived very different lives.

In the Afrikaans language, *apartheid* means "apartness."

Soweto, the African living area of Johannesburg, under apartheid

Indian Inspiration

Mandela read about and admired Mohandas Gandhi. Gandhi fought for the rights of Indians in South Africa. He also worked in India for the same kind of changes as Mandela. Gandhi wanted peace for his people in India and other countries. He taught that instead of being violent and hateful, people should solve conflicts with peaceful actions. Though he never met Gandhi, Mandela was inspired by this idea. He also wanted to change laws peacefully.

Peaceful Is Productive

Researchers have studied whether violent struggles or peaceful struggles are more successful. The answer is clear.

25% Successful

75% Successful

Violent

Peaceful

Mandela called Gandhi the "Sacred Warrior."

"In a world riven by violence and strife, Gandhi's message of peace and non-violence holds the key to human survival in the 21st century."

—Nelson Mandela

Political Action

Mandela joined the ANC. In his political work, he met many people pushing for change. Mandela used these meetings to plan **strikes** and boycotts. He wanted people to protest the laws that kept Africans from having rights.

The government didn't like what the ANC said or did. They **banned** Mandela from being anywhere with more than one person at a time. And if he left the capital, he would be arrested. The government wanted to keep him from traveling. The ban made it hard for him to work with others. They hoped this would keep him from influencing so many people. But the threats didn't stop Mandela. He continued to work as a lawyer and activist.

Helping the Cause

At the ANC, Mandela led the Defiance Campaign. He organized protests against unjust laws around the country. The ANC grew to include from 7,000 to over 100,000 members. His work angered the government, and he was arrested.

Freedom Charter

In 1955, the ANC had a large meeting, but Mandela could not attend. Many people worked together to create the Freedom Charter, which listed the things they wanted to change in the government. Even though he was not there, Mandela was asked for his ideas. It was an important step in creating a fair and equal government.

activists campaigning

Raise Your Voice

Nelson Mandela is famous for taking a stand. He believed everyone should have a voice. Do you have something to say? You can write a letter to someone in the government, such as a governor or senator. Or you can write to a magazine or newspaper so your ideas are published for thousands to read. Protests are also effective. You can follow Mandela's lead with these steps.

Step 1

Decide what your message will be. Perhaps you want more books for the library or bins for recycling. You must be prepared to explain why your cause is important.

Step 2

Spread the word to anyone who will listen. In order to make an impact, you need to have a lot of people supporting you. Spread the word by handing out fliers. Encourage others to share your message.

Step 3

Ask adults, like teachers and parents, to support you. If they believe in your ideas, they can talk to school officials or neighbors for you.

Step 4

Make posters for your protest. Make them easy to understand with pictures and big, clear letters. Hang signs around school or in the neighborhood. The more people who are aware of your cause, the more people who can help make changes.

Step 5

Compromise is an important part of any protest. You've worked hard to get to this point. Now you need to talk with the other side about ways you can come to an agreement. You'll know you've been successful when you're both excited for the future.

Political Action

The government watched Mandela closely. They looked for ways to stop him. They wanted to prevent people from organizing. They wanted to protect apartheid.

In 1956, Mandela was arrested. He was charged with **treason**. There was little evidence. But it was an easy way to silence him. The trial lasted four years. Mandela was found to be innocent. But he knew he could no longer work in the open. He went into hiding.

Mandela was upset. Progress wasn't being made fast enough. The government would not listen to peaceful protests. In 1960, police killed 69 unarmed African protestors. Africans were still being treated cruelly. And the whites in power did little to help them.

While in hiding, Mandela and his fellow activists tried a new approach. They created the Spear of the Nation. It was the military side of the ANC. The group carried out acts of **sabotage** (SAB-uh-tahzh). They were desperate to end apartheid.

Mandela and others raise their fists in defiance as they are taken to prison.

Fighting Together

Mandela's second wife, Winnie, believed many of the same things that Mandela did. During this time, she also joined the ANC. Today, she is known by many as the Mother of the Nation.

The Spear of the Nation used violent as well as peaceful actions to attract attention. Here, they have pulled down an electrical-power station.

23

Life Underground

To avoid the government, Mandela went into hiding. He was able to avoid the police by never staying in one place too long. But the ANC needed a place to meet secretly.

Front of Main Building

The police called Mandela "The Black Pimpernel" because he always escaped. They got the name from *The Scarlet Pimpernel,* a novel about a French man who always avoided capture.

Nelson Mandela's room on Liliesleaf farm

When the police investigated, they thought it was a white man's farm and that Mandela was a servant.

For two years, the ANC used Liliesleaf Farm to store weapons, print freedom literature, and broadcast radio programs.

Thatched Cottage

Veld Road to Secret Gate

Combi

Water Tanks

Taunus Panel Van

Outhouses

Mandela wore disguises, including dressing as a driver, a gardener, and a cook, to avoid detection.

Political Prisoner

In 1962, Mandela traveled illegally to speak about freedom. Soon after his return, he was arrested. He was found guilty and sentenced to five years in prison.

While in jail, Mandela and his friends were charged with sabotage. They were sentenced to life in prison. They sometimes stopped eating to protest. But in time, Mandela had to give in. If he refused to eat, he would die. In his heart, he wanted to end apartheid. He knew all South Africans deserved better. The government wanted Mandela in jail. They wanted to make him give up. But the plan didn't work. Instead, it made Mandela more passionate. He knew how cruel life was for Africans. But he believed, if he kept trying, he could make South Africa a better place.

Words of Peace

At his trial, Mandela spoke these words of wisdom:

"I have fought against white domination, and I have fought against black domination. I have cherished the **ideal** of a democratic and free society in which all persons live together in harmony and with equal opportunities. It is an ideal which I hope to live for and to achieve. But if needs be, it is an ideal for which I am prepared to die."

Prison Life

Mandela's prison cell was only seven square feet. Every six months, he was allowed one letter. It could be no more than 500 words long. He could see his family only once every six months. He had a uniform, a mat to sleep on, and two blankets.

the entrance to Robben Island prison

Mandela was sent to Robben Island prison. He was forced to work under tough conditions. Sometimes, the prison didn't give him the letters or books that were sent to him. He was forced to live in a small, harsh cell.

Mandela and five of his friends, including Sisulu, were all sentenced to life in prison. They taught other prisoners about politics and the law. Even in prison, many people still looked up to Mandela. They believed the same things he did. They believed that all people should have equal rights. They admired Mandela's **integrity**. He stayed true to his beliefs even when he was being treated badly. He promised to fight for freedom until the end of his days.

46664

Mandela had another name. He was known by his prison number 46664. Today, his number is a **symbol** of freedom around the world.

Mandela University

Prison was a difficult place, but Mandela wanted to show the other prisoners that even harsh treatment couldn't change his beliefs. He tried to be the best person he could be even in the darkest moments. He led prisoners to ask for changes in the prison. He was able to help other prisoners win better food and access to music. Robben Island was often called *The University* because of how much the prisoners learned from Mandela and the other activists there.

Nelson Mandela and Sisulu in prison on Robben Island.

Chapter 3

Freedom

People around the world agreed that South Africans were not being treated fairly. Many countries asked that Mandela be freed. They passed laws to pressure South Africa to change. But South Africa's government ignored the world. They would not end apartheid.

By 1985, there were many problems in the country. People were **rioting**. There was great unhappiness. The government tried to gain Mandela's support in prison. They offered Mandela freedom. In exchange, he would have to allow apartheid to continue. But he told them, "Only free men can **negotiate**." He stood for all South Africans. He would not help the government unless all people would be free.

anti-apartheid protestors

Anti-apartheid protestors march against the government.

Money Matters

There was big money to be made by musicians who were willing to travel to perform in South Africa during the apartheid years. Many famous artists refused to play in South Africa until the laws changed. Bruce Springsteen, Miles Davis, and Run-DMC were among those who refused to perform there.

"It is never my custom to use words lightly. If 27 years in prison have done anything to us, it was to...make us understand how precious words are and how real speech is in its impact on the way people live and die."

—Nelson Mandela

Free Mandela!

Mandela may have been imprisoned, but he was never alone. The whole world worked together to set him free. He was and continues to be a symbol of freedom.

The United Nations

In 1964, South Africa could no longer take part in the General Assembly at the United Nations. The United Nations strongly supported Mandela's release from prison.

"It is in your hands to make of our world a better one."

—Nelson Mandela

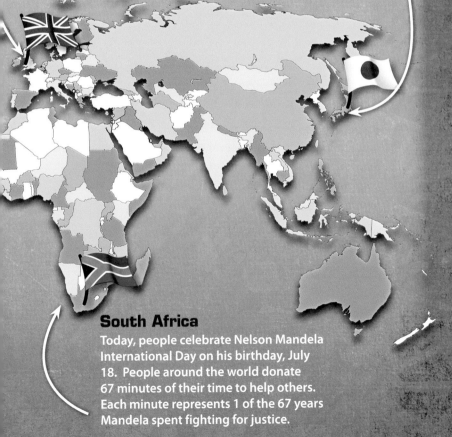

England

In 1988, England hosted a huge concert for Mandela's 70th birthday. He was still in jail, but 75,000 people came to the concert. The concert was shown on television in 64 countries. The jail received 11 bags of birthday cards for Mandela.

Japan

In 1964, South Africa was banned from the Olympic Games in Tokyo, Japan. South Africa was allowed to participate in the Olympics only after Mandela was released.

South Africa

Today, people celebrate Nelson Mandela International Day on his birthday, July 18. People around the world donate 67 minutes of their time to help others. Each minute represents 1 of the 67 years Mandela spent fighting for justice.

A Hard Road Ahead

When he was released, Mandela walked hand in hand with his wife. It was the first time Mandela had been seen outside prison in 27 years. He gave many speeches after his release. In them, he always reminded people that there is "no easy walk to freedom."

Freedom for All

In 1986, Mandela began talking with members of the government. He later met with Frederick Willem de Klerk (VILL-em da KLERK), the president of South Africa. De Klerk had been listening to the world's calls for change. Mandela believed de Klerk wanted to end apartheid. On February 11, 1990, Mandela was finally released from prison. Crowds of people around the world gathered to watch. As he walked out of the prison, he held his fist in the air. It was a powerful symbol of his struggle for freedom.

Mandela urged all people to think about peace. He knew not everyone would agree on how to run the country. In a speech he said, "Now is the time...to stand together against those who...wish to destroy...the freedom of all of us." He wanted people to avoid **prejudice**. He wanted them to think about what was best for the country.

A New Day

When Mandela was released from prison, it meant apartheid was coming to an end. Black and white South Africans were able to live and work together rather than separately. The country had been divided for many years. With Mandela's freedom, the whole country was free to build a new future.

Mandela speaks to supporters under the ANC flag after his release from prison.

DIG DEEPER!

Peaceful Protests

The members of the ANC used a sign. It was a fist raised in the air. It meant they were fighting for freedom. It meant they would fight using words, silence, or stillness. But the fist in the air also meant they would not use violence. Do you recognize these other peaceful symbols?

Ancient Romans used the olive branch as a symbol of Pax, the goddess of peace. She was believed to bring olive branches to those at war.

White doves often symbolize peace. Churches, artists, and writers have all used this symbol.

What do you think symbolizes peace?

This peace sign was designed to protest weapons and war.

People often raise two fingers in the form of a *V* to symbolize peace. Protesters used the sign to stand for peace and changed the meaning. Originally, the *V* stood for victory.

Presidents and Partners

Mandela and de Klerk worked together for two years. Sometimes, they agreed. But sometimes, they did not. Each worked to see the other person's side. It wasn't always easy. But they were dedicated to the idea of democracy. In 1993, a new **constitution** was created. It made apartheid illegal. For the first time, all South Africans, black and white, had equal rights.

Mandela and de Klerk accepting their Nobel Peace Prize

A Noble Moment

In 1993, Mandela and de Klerk were awarded the Nobel Peace Prize for their work. A Nobel Prize is the highest honor a person can earn. Together, they brought freedom and peace to their country. Many people were amazed that these two very different people were able to work together.

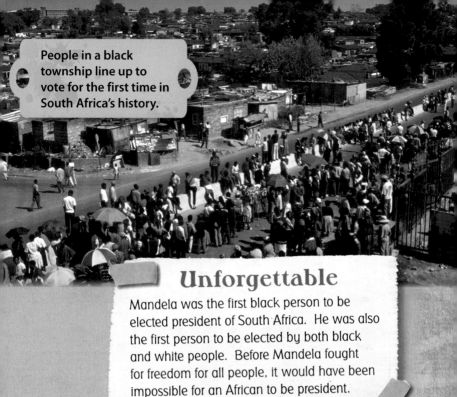

People in a black township line up to vote for the first time in South Africa's history.

Unforgettable

Mandela was the first black person to be elected president of South Africa. He was also the first person to be elected by both black and white people. Before Mandela fought for freedom for all people, it would have been impossible for an African to be president.

In 1994, the country held its first democratic election. The people elected Mandela to be their country's president. He was 75 years old. When he took office, he held hands with de Klerk. A black man and a white man stood together. Their joined hands were raised in the air. Mandela knew all the years he had spent alone in jail had been worth it.

Today, Mandela speaks out for peace. He inspires leaders around the world. His message is the same as it has been for many years. We all deserve peace. We all deserve equal rights. We all deserve freedom.

DIG DEEPER!

Time Line of Nelson Mandela's Life

1918
Born in South Africa

1925
Starts primary school

1940
Stages student protest at Fort Hare University

1961
Goes into hiding

1964
Sentenced to life in prison and sent to Robben Island

"I was an ordinary man who became a leader because of extraordinary circumstances."

—Nelson Mandela

1944
Attends first ANC meeting

1952
Leads the Defiance Campaign

1956
Arrested for treason

1990
Released from prison

1993
Wins Nobel Peace Prize with de Klerk

1994
Elected president of South Africa in the country's first free election

41

Glossary

ancestry—the family members that came before someone

apartheid—a law that allowed Afrikaners to treat Africans in cruel and unfair ways

banned—stopped someone by law from doing something

boycotted—refused to buy from a person, organization, or country

constitution—a list of laws and rules that a government agrees to follow

democracy—a type of government in which all adults have a say about how the government works

equality—when all people have the same amount of power

ideal—a person, thing, or idea that many people think is perfect

integrity—the quality of being honest and sincere

minority—a group of people who have a different background or religion than most people in a country

negotiate—to compromise with another person to reach an agreement

peaceful protest—to argue or fight for something in a nonviolent way

prejudice—to judge another person based on how they are different, often because of racial or religious differences

rioting—publicly acting in violence

royals—people with royal roots; kings, queens, or others who rule

sabotage—a disruption of the work and services used by people

segregation—separation based on race or class

strikes—refusals to work or complete work until those in charge make changes

symbol—something that stands for something else

treason—to willingly do something that will hurt your country

Index

Bibliography

Koosman, Melissa. *Meet Our New Student from South Africa*. Mitchell Lane Publishers, 2009.

  This book tells of a third-grade class that is getting ready for a new student from South Africa by learning about his country's history, languages, recipes, plants, and animals.

Nelson Mandela Foundation, The. *Nelson Mandela: The Authorized Comic Book*. W. W. Norton & Company, 2009.

  Explore the life of Nelson Mandela from his childhood to his life as the president of South Africa, in this comic-book-style biography.

Oluonye, Mary N. *South Africa (Country Explorers)*. Lerner Publications Company, 2008.

  Learn more about South Africa's land, people, climate, animals, food, school, religion, and more in this colorful book.

Rice, Dona. William Rice. *Mohandas Gandhi*. Teacher Created Materials, 2011.

  During a difficult time in India's history, Gandhi learned many lessons about how to be gentle and honorable. Find out how these lessons helped him become one of the world's greatest leaders.

More to Explore

Apartheid Museum

http://www.apartheidmuseum.org/comics

Two comics take a present-day South African boy back in time to witness protests and riots.

Kid World Citizen

http://kidworldcitizen.org

This website has activites that help you think about people and cultures around the world. For more information on Nelson Mandela, type *Nelson Mandela* into the search box.

Nelson Mandela Centre of Memory

http://www.nelsonmandela.org

Scroll down under the *Multimedia resources* tab and click on images and video to view photos and footage of Mandela and the people of South Africa.

South Africa Games and Activities for Kids

http://www.wartgames.com/themes/countries/southafrica.html

This site has links to fun facts, folktales, recipes, and more from South Africa.

About the Author

Tamara Leigh Hollingsworth was born and raised in Cupertino, California. She attended Hollins University, where she earned a degree in English. She has been a high school English teacher for many years. She currently lives in Atlanta, Georgia. When she is not working with her beloved students, Tamara loves to spend time with her husband, her daughter, and her books—especially biographies.